The Knock that Opened Years

poems by

Marcia Blacker

Finishing Line Press
Georgetown, Kentucky

The Knock that Opened Years

Copyright © 2018 by Marcia Blacker
ISBN 978-1-63534-812-5 First Edition
All rights reserved under International and Pan-American Copyright Conventions. No part of this book may be reproduced in any manner whatsoever without written permission from the publisher, except in the case of brief quotations embodied in critical articles and reviews.

ACKNOWLEDGMENTS

Grateful acknowledgements to the following publications where these poems first appeared or received honors.

India U.S.A. Connecting Communities: Kettle; Mother Earth
Lite Baltimore's Literary Newspaper: Making Progress?
PKA'S Advocate: Knock
Poetica Magazine: Reflections of Jewish Thought: Bonds of Friendship; Honey of My Faith
St. Joseph's Messenger: Bonds of Friendship
The Awakenings Review: Knitting Through the Years
The Oak: Dementia Strikes; honorable mention in Rhyme Time Contest
The Pegasus Review: Bonds of Friendship

Publisher: Leah Maines
Editor: Christen Kincaid
Cover Art and Design: Karen Collidge; www.karencollidge.com
Author Photo: Karen Collidge; www.karencollidge.com

Printed in the USA on acid-free paper.
Order online: www.finishinglinepress.com
        also available on amazon.com

Author inquiries and mail orders:
Finishing Line Press
P. O. Box 1626
Georgetown, Kentucky 40324
U. S. A.

Table of Contents

Bonds of Friendship 1
Honey of My Faith 2
Knitting through the Years 3
Stroll by the Sea 4
The Game 5
Prayer by the Sea 6
Gifts 7
Winter's Prayer of Hope 8
Winter's Miracle 9
Painted Palate 10
Knock 11
Fishermate's Yarn 12
Dementia My Love 13
Dementia Strikes 14
Why? 15
The Kettle 16
Wine Goblets at Passover 17
We Once Knew a Fisherman 18
Nicky 20
Bailey the Service Dog 21
Hear Our Prayer 22
Making Progress? 23
A Prayer of Thanks 24
Mother Earth 25
Poet's Garden 26
The Pretzel 27
My Special One 28

Dedicated to my dearest friend, Phyllis Rubin

*In memory of my husband, Barry Lee Blacker,
my sister-in-law, Lois Sinofsky
and my dear Aunt Rose.
Their encouragement and love
helped make this work possible.*

*To Karen Collidge Cappeluto
for her wonderful cover art
and photography.*

BONDS OF FRIENDSHIP

My friend and I sit side by side.
My Mom, her Mom across the table,
taken back to another table,
another year, another cloth,
laden with lace, and challah and wine.

My friend and I listen
as her Papa spoke of the Rabbi's sermon,
how we, the Chosen ones,
have suffered and survived
all these years.

And we two girls, young in spirit,
young in mind,
sat and listened,
sipping wine, the blood red juice
that grown-ups sipped,
melting away barriers,
bonding as with cement
our ties from youth.

And we four break bread
not wanting this meeting to end,
reminiscent of a time long ago
Across the cloth
As years drift by.

HONEY OF MY FAITH

Phyllis poured the honey into my faith,
honey like mortar, cementing my Jewish bricks together.

Sitting at the table on Yom Kippur day,
my dad, a gentle, intelligent soul,
but not that day inclined to pray.

One hand holding a forbidden sandwich,
the other, a pen scratching wise words on a slate,
so involved, oblivious of the holy date.
The front door open wide,
with nothing, no nothing to hide.

Phyllis, my friend, sharing with me
her Bat Mitzvah legacy,
her Rabbi's sermons,
her Yom Kippur traditions
pouring the honey of Jewish faith
down the parched throat of my neglected Jewish soul.

KNITTING THROUGH THE YEARS

Knitting needles click
The hourglass turns
Sand sifts slowly through time
Evy's fingers busy, knit one, pearl two
Friends and neighbors surround her
The ritual, an evening of cheerful camaraderie clicks on.

Lois enters
Another room, another time
Other busy needles click on
Smiling faces welcome her as she enters
Suddenly a vision, her mother's knitting group
Another time long ago,
Dances before her eyes,
She hesitates in the doorway,
A tear trickling down her cheek
She brushes it away
Finds an empty seat and begins, knit one, pearl two
The sound of busy needles clicks on
The sand in the hourglass sifting slowly through the years.

STROLL BY THE SEA

Step after step by the sea in the sun
Lois and I amble along
Arm in arm we feel we belong
Skirting ocean's salty spray
I feel inclined to kneel and pray.

My mind's eye drifts back in time
My Ema, Abba, Lois and I
Holding hands, jumping waves
Foamy bubbles tickling toes
Splashing sea anointing nose
Giggles building from within
We wish this time would never end.

Once again Lois and I stroll along
Reminiscing our old familiar song
Thank you Hashem for this another stroll by the sea
And for giving me a sister-in-law more like a sister to me.

THE GAME

The ball rolls towards baby's feet
I bend to retrieve it.
Baby's gaze follows
All wide-eyed with innocence and anticipation.

I grin down at him, my boy.
My mother's eyes smiling back at me
Warm, but mellow
Like a vintage wine
All steeped in a wisdom coming from
A delicate mixture of life's joys and pain.

A drop of wet dribbles down baby's chin
A tear down mine.

Baby grins up at me.
I release the ball.
The game begins again.

PRAYER BY THE SEA

Ocean blue,
Waves rolling in,
Fish a jumping
See their fins

Little children
Wiggle toes
Squishing sand
Hold their nose

Jumping high
Ocean spray
Means to me
A time to pray

Standing there
Salty air
Blows my hair
Oh Lord, Hear my prayer

So near to G-d
I feel renewed.

GIFTS

A baby world lifts up its head
Of roses pink and white.

As Mother Nature showers down
Her rain of golden light.

As dew drops crown the velvet grass,
And pansies all but quiver,

G-d above beholds the scene
For He alone the giver.

WINTER'S PRAYER OF HOPE

Winter drapes its cloak on morrow's morn
Sprinkling earth with icy white
Above, the sky's blanket of gray
Hides yesterday's innocence at play.

But deep within temple walls
Where pious souls bend and sway
Weary hearts pulsate as they pray
For peace across a divided earth
For wars to cease their chilling dearth
Of harmony of man
From land to land
Across sea and sand.

Oh please our Lord help to end these brutal wars
Opening wide more peaceful, prayerful doors
Where snow white birds surround the ark
With hope and love piercing every heart.

WINTER'S MIRACLE

Storm winds wail
Throughout the night.

Snowy silhouettes draped
In robes of white.

Snow-laden branches bow
As if in prayer.

Winter's miracle returns
For all to share.

PAINTED PALETTE

Winter drapes its cloak of silent lace
Lovers cling together through the night
Snowflakes proudly paint earth's peaceful face

Through empty miles of empty space
Children dream of Rudolf's nose's light
Winter drapes its cloak of silent lace

Mounds of white increase but not in haste
Giant grizzlies snoring out of sight
Snowflakes proudly paint earth's peaceful face

Playful paws swat the pillowcase
Lazy kittens snuggle by the fire bright
Winter drapes its cloak of silent lace

Tree limbs bend from head to waist
Toddlers sailing planes on snow-bound flights
Snowflakes proudly paint earth's peaceful face.

A world now covered with angelic paste
A frosty white tranquil sight
Winter drapes its cloak of silent lace
Snowflakes proudly paint earth's peaceful face.

KNOCK

A knock
The door opens
He steps in
After only three months
The camera clicks
A bird in flight
Frozen like the freckled face that caught my heart.

The door opens
I think I love you stings my face
Shoots through me like an arrow.

I blink, too stunned to answer.
I offer grapes and wine.
Munching, we sit and pine
Knight takes rook, check mate,
He wins again.

The game continues twenty-three years
Summers in the sand, waves lifting our bodies in unison
Spring, fall, on the pier tossing lines in the sea
As birds depart.
Winter dawns, we two trudge through snow
As we age, daring fate to keep the gate open
A while longer
The door,
The knock that opened years.

FISHERMATE'S YARN

Upon the pier we swing and sway,
Wavy nibbles are at play.
Keeping secrets shared, we pine.
Memories weaving through my mind.

Above, a dove in winged flight
Soars as my love casts for a bite.
Upon the pier each sunny noon,
We two spoon as on our honeymoon.

Reeling in a trophy fish
Is my love's unending wish.
For basking in the sun, he is king.
Casting the rod, hearing the reel sing.

But all too soon, fish swim downstream
As time retreats from our summer's dream.
Yet end of season brings its charm
As we two await our next fishermate's yarn.

DEMENTIA MY LOVE

He extended his hand
Like the anchor to a ship tossing at sea,
To grasp, and pull myself up on.
Up, up out of a quagmire of confusion,
Where my mind spun like a loose spoke of a broken wheel.

But now the spokes are tightening.
My mind clears, but our hands, our grip, begins to slip.

Like a seesaw pivoting on its axle,
He declines,
Like the chipping away of time,
Numbers, words evade him,
Ordinary street signs, foggy like the early morning haze.

But our fingers barely meet now.
Sleep comes quickly to him.
But I lie awake thinking
How long? How long?

DEMENTIA STRIKES

Like a tiger's silent paws,
Creeping stealthily into the night,
Eyes gleaming, staring, fixed upon you,
Until it's too late to halt its pounce.

With the full force of a silent bomb's
Explosion into the air,
Shattering pieces of thought
In every direction.

Mindfulness, memories, flying like
Bits of debris,
Tiny remnants of a mind's steel turret
That once was.

WHY?

His final curtain drops
Leaving no room for tomorrows.

Bread and jam remain.
Marmalade memories spread over my mind.

Trousers draped across the chair.
How dare he leave them there?

Blue coffee tin
A shade upon the lamp
My husband's signature stamp.

Why?

A mind too weary to reply.
Can anyone tell me why?

My eyelids droop
Sleep bringing him home to me once more.

THE KETTLE

I sup a sip of honey
Green Chamomile tea with mint
Recalling the warn threads of time
Lips apart on the rim
Like lips parted years ago
In the heat of the night
But the kettle's whistle no longer sings.
Our steam long gone
My lips upon the rim of gold.

WINE GOBLETS AT PASSOVER

Across the rims of time
Why is this night different from all other nights?
Years gone by my husband reclined next to me
Surrounded by aunts and cousins from two to ninety-three

Around the lace clad cloth laden with matzah and wine
He sipped from each goblet one at a time
Then the youngest child recited the four questions
My husband sipped a little more.

His spirit dancing around the rims of time
I raise my goblet to my lips
Sipping the sad sweet taste of memories vintage past
I am blessed.

WE ONCE KNEW A FISHERMAN

We once knew a fisherman
Short, stocky and gray
And sadly to say
With a bald spot to stay.

But sitting alone
On his favorite rocking chair
His world was like heaven
Without worry or care.

There carefully sorting
Bobbers, weights and fishing hooks
He cared not at all
How long the job took.

Then gathering rods,
Both left handed and right,
He inserted the line
And turned the reel tight.

Then from patio door
This fisherman departed
So free, so joyful and
And so light hearted,

To face the challenge of
Waters both shallow and deep,
To bring home some fish,
Some fresh fish to keep.

We once knew a fisherman
Who knew his true call
Through spring and summer
And into the fall.

To sit in the breeze
And bask in the light
With great anticipation
Of snagging a bite.

So now as we gather
To say our good-by
We pray dear Lord
In heaven up high

Please grant Barry peace
And comfort his soul
And send him our prayers
In heaven's fishing hole.

For there he is king
Holding his grand fishing rod
Please send him our love,
Dear Almighty G-d.

NICKY

Nicky, now thirteen,
By Canine measure ninety-one
Going on forever
Loyal, mine to care for
White paws at the door
Of my raw open wounds,
A cool moist nose
To heal the hurts.

BAILEY THE SERVICE DOG

Bailey Jackson loved by all
Not too tall, rather small
With her creamy white curls
And short pudgy tail
She visits us daily,
Never to fail.
Greeting residents relaxing in the TV Room
of our own Assisted Living Home,
We welcome her joyfully,
To us she's well known.

She waddles after folks with walkers and canes.
Follow the leader her favorite game.

Nibbling crumbs from off the floor
She raises her paw begging for more.

She loves you to pet her
And offer doggie treats.
Once enticed, she's glued to your feet.

Then "Bailey Jackson," her mother calls
As Bailey looks wistfully trying to stall.

With a wag of her stubby little tail
She woofs as if to say, "I really like being here today."

HEAR OUR PRAYER

Go back three giant steps
To a simpler world

Where Flubadub won
Children's hearts

And youthful voices shouted,
"It's Howdy Doodie Time."

Dear Lord, I do believe
We've lost our way.

With guns and shots
We've gone astray.

Please help us Dear Lord
To treat all as our own,

Before nothing is left
But skeleton and bone.

We must relearn to
Trust one another

And stop, forever,
Killing our brother.

Go back three giant steps,
If that's what it takes,

To open our eyes all the way
And stop making these awful mistakes.

MAKING PROGRESS?

How far have we strayed
From days gone by

When dew drops landing
On lily white petals
Gave joy and delight,

When Zeus and Hercules
Held no mystery for great minds

And a fluttering fire-fly's flight
Still held its mark
In man's daily journal of pleasures

When dreams met reality
To share in the consummation
Of conscious and unconscious minds?

How long before
The burning flames die,

Leaving behind soot and residue
Where robots rule
By pressing plastic buttons

And frozen faces
Rule the earth?

A PRAYER OF THANKS

G-d's miracles, his creations
Far beyond man's measure
No mathematical equations
Can ever measure
The speed of clouds
Drifting high through the sky
A silhouette of the unknown.

What to make of G-d's artistry
His portraits
A stroke of His breath from a vacuum
Creating the whole world in six days,
The seventh to rest on?

Can we humans ever try
To understand His creations,
Vibrant greens like the meadow's queen
Splashed across the earth?
A cineramic vision
Surrounding the human scene.

Or, shall we simply rejoice
Hearing His heavenly voice,
Reciting daily prayers of thanks
To Hashem, our Maker?

MOTHER EARTH

The beat, beat, beating of drums
Men crouched in a circle
Palms extended downward to feel the
Thawing earth beneath their skin.

As rising sun showers rays of light
Strength is born from this cold night.
Upon the earth there glows a crown
Proud young braves look forward bound.

One dream,
One heart,
One spirit, renewed each day
As mother earth guides the way.

POET'S GARDEN

Poems asleep below the surface
Like seeds under earth
Awaiting a dousing of rain
To awaken them.
Pages turn.
Words swirling like daffodils
Swaying in the rays of golden sun.
My poem swelling into blossoms,
Bursts into bloom.

THE PRETZEL

Words twisting like a pretzel
Sapping the juices of many tongues
Tumbling upside down
The acrobat awakens
Touching endless hidden treasures
In a mind's roving maze
Through the haze of spins and turns
Mumbo jumbo becomes a gem
To savor like a wine poured from a
Flask of space to eternity.

MY SPECIAL ONE

I may not always tie my shoes
Or keep my numbers straight
Sometimes the six comes before the five
As if it can hardly wait.

And as I try to say the date
But just cannot remember
The days and months get all mixed up
With November following December.

But, my morning sun shines in just as strong
My apple tastes as sweet
And as I reach to shake a branch
It drops down by my feet.

As evening's curtain gently lowers
And I begin to nod
A loving spirit touches me
With treasures sent from G-d.

Marcia Blacker was born and raised in Baltimore, Maryland. She holds a B. S. Degree from Towson State College and a Master's Equivalency in Education. She taught young children for over twenty years.

Marcia has been widowed for twenty years. Her interests include reading and writing, listening to music, painting pottery, exercising and working with an autistic teenager. She also enjoys socializing with old and new friends and family.

Marcia has enjoyed the power of words for most of her life. Her poetry has been published in *PKA's Advocate, Poetica Magazine, Reflections of Jewish Thought, St. Joseph's Messenger, The Oak, The Awakenings Review, The Pegasus Review* and others. Her poem "Dementia Strikes" received Honorable Mention in the *Rhyme Time* Poetry Contest, and her poem, "Bonds of Friendship" was a winner in the Phyllis McLaines Contest.

Marcia is very proud to have her first collection of poems published by the Finishing Line Press.

www.ingramcontent.com/pod-product-compliance
Lightning Source LLC
LaVergne TN
LVHW041513070426
835507LV00012B/1551